Strategies to Create Lifetime Income for Baby Boomers

PLANNING TO MAKE YOUR SAVINGS LAST AS LONG
AS YOU DO ... REGARDLESS OF HOW LONG YOU
LIVE, WHAT DIRECTION THE MARKET TAKES, OR
WHAT HAPPENS IN THE ECONOMY OVERALL

By Artie Bernaducci
and Denny Frasiolas

Copyright © 2021 Artie Bernaducci and Denny Frasiolas. All rights reserved.

Advisory services are offered through Retirement Income Advisory Group, LLC, a Registered Investment Advisor in the state of New Jersey. Insurance products and services are offered through its affiliated companies, All Access Brokerage, LLC, d/b/a Medicare Supplement Store and The Retiring Baby Boomer Group LLC. None of these companies are affiliated with or endorsed by the Social Security Administration or any government agency.

The contents of this book are provided for informational purposes only and are not intended to serve as the basis for any financial decisions. Any tax, legal, or estate planning information is general in nature. It should not be construed as legal or tax advice. Always consult an attorney or tax professional regarding the applicability of this information to your unique situation.

Information presented is believed to be factual and up-to-date, but we do not guarantee its accuracy, and it should not be regarded as a complete analysis of the subjects discussed. All expressions of opinion are those of the author as of the date of publication and are subject to change. Content should not be construed as personalized investment advice, nor should it be interpreted as an offer to buy or sell any securities mentioned. A financial advisor should be consulted before implementing any of the strategies presented.

Investing involves risk, including the potential loss of principal. No investment strategy can guarantee a profit or protect against loss in periods of declining values. Any references to protection benefits or guaranteed/lifetime income streams refer only to fixed insurance products, not securities or investment products. Insurance and annuity product guarantees are backed by the financial strength and claims-paying ability of the issuing insurance company.

This publication is licensed to the individual reader only. Duplication or distribution by any means, including email, disk, photocopy, and recording, to a person other than the original purchaser, is a violation of international copyright law.

Publisher:

**Retirement Income Advisory Group, LLC,
1460 Route 9 N, Suite 210 A,
Woodbridge, NJ 07095
www.Retire-USA.com**

Strategies to Create Lifetime Income for Baby Boomers by Artie Bernaducci and Denny Frasiolas

ISBN: 979852121277551

While they have made every effort to verify the information provided in this publication, neither the authors nor the publisher assumes any responsibility for errors in, omissions from, or different interpretations of the subject matter.

The information herein may be subject to varying laws and practices in different areas, states, and countries. The reader assumes all responsibility for use of the information.

Special Invitation from the Authors

Please email info@retire-usa.com
or call (732) 455-9990

To help you get maximum value from this book, we have three gifts for you.

First, we have retirement white papers written by Artie and will send you whatever three you would like.

To receive them, send an email to info@Retire-USA, and in the subject line please put "WHITE PAPERS."

We will snail mail or email them to you. Just let us know your preference and which three you'd like. (Include your address in the email if you want them mailed).

The white papers are:

- *How to Secure Divorced Spouse's & Widow/Widower's Benefits from Social Security*

- *The Power of Retirement Income Unleashed*
- *Is Your IOU to the IRS Growing?*
- *How to Prepare for Your Changing Financial Needs in Retirement*
- *Baby Boomers: 48 Ways to Stop an Identity Thief*
- *The Baby Boomers Financial Guide to Getting Through the COVID-19 Pandemic*
- *The Retiring Baby Boomer Needs A Plan to Retire*
- *Keeping Your Savings Immune from Long-Term Care Expenses*

Second, we will send you a hard copy of our fun to read monthly newsletter, *The BOOMERANG* for six months.

Lastly, you can have a twenty-nine-minute consultation with either author to discuss any questions you may have about retirement.

PS:

There also is a lot more to find
on the Resources tab at
www.Retire-USA.com
and on our podcast at
www.RetirementAfter60.com

Table of Contents

INTRODUCTION
How Big Is Your Retirement Shortfall? vii

CHAPTER ONE
Planning Means Being Prepared 1

CHAPTER TWO
Where Are You On the Mountain? 5

CHAPTER THREE
Accumulation vs. Distribution 13
    The Right Distribution Plan Makes a Difference....15
    Do You Have the Right Type of Guide?................20

CHAPTER FOUR
Avoid Common Income Planning Mistakes 25
    Are You Using the Right Tools? 26

CHAPTER FIVE
Recreating a Paycheck.................................33
    Social Security.. 34
    Pension... 36

    Annuities 38
    Dividend Income 46
    Interest-Only Withdrawals 49
    Liquidate Assets 52
    The Time-Based Segmentation System 56
    The Bottom Line on Recreating a Paycheck 61

CHAPTER SIX
Case Study Retirement 63

CHAPTER SEVEN
Taking the Next Step 89

About Retirement Income Advisory Group 95
    Our Mission 96

About Artie Bernaducci 97
About Denny Frasiolas 101

The Purpose of This Book

Today, with people living longer than ever before in history, one of the biggest concerns on the minds of retirees and baby boomers is running out of income in retirement.

Running out of money in retirement is the No. 1 concern of many Americans. Only 20 percent of people are worried about dying, but 58 percent worry about not having enough income in retirement.[1]

While there is no easy fix to address a person's concerns, often having a plan in place—a written plan that addresses the specific causes of your

---

[1] Stephen Chen. Forbes. October 20, 2019. "This Simple Step Can Address Your #1 Retirement Fear."
https://www.forbes.com/sites/stephenchen/2019/10/20/people-are-3x-more-worried-about-their-1-financial-fear-than-dying/#4e29f8121576.

concern—can help reduce worry about the unknown or unpredictable by making them known and predictable. This guide will provide you with the strategies to help you:

• Build your lifetime income plan, so you don't run out at the time you need it most.

• Protect yourself against the financial risks that can deplete your retirement savings.

• Ensure you have an income strategy custom-designed for your specific needs and goals.

As baby boomers like me are retiring and getting ready to retire, they will spend whatever it takes—and they're the wealthiest generation in our country—to make themselves live an enjoyable life in their retirement years.

David Rubinstein

Philanthropist and financier

Source: Glasbergen Cartoon Service.
https://glasbergen.com

INTRODUCTION

How Big Is Your Retirement Shortfall?

According to the U.S. Bureau of Labor Statistics' current population survey, the percentage of Americans over sixty-five who have continued to work has doubled since 1985. That means 10.6 million retirement-age workers are still employed or are looking for employment.[2]

Why is that?

---

[2] Lincoln Plews. CapitalOne. April 22, 2019. "Older Americans in the Workforce." https://unitedincome.capitalone.com/library/older-americans-in-the-workforce.

One reason could be too many people are reaching retirement age with less money in the bank than they need to pay their bills.

Is that you?

Today, people are living longer than ever before in history. For a number of reasons, this is great news. It can mean more time spent with family and friends, more time traveling, and more time to enjoy life after retirement.

> *The average life expectancy of people in the United States has risen to 78.8 in recent years compared to an average lifetime of 69.9 years in 1960.*[3]

Unfortunately, it also means our savings will have to last longer—in some cases, much longer. Because of our longer life spans, savings, and investments we used to only need for a few years after we left the workforce are now having to be stretched out for twenty, thirty, or even more years.

---

[3] Aaron O'Neill. Statista. Feb. 3, 2021. "Life expectancy in the United States, 1860-2020."
https://www.statista.com/statistics/1040079/life-expectancy-united-states-all-time/.

How can this be accomplished, especially with today's volatile stock market, historically low interest rates, and ongoing inflation?

The answer—by having a good income plan.

While many of us may be saving for the future, what most people don't realize is saving and investing for retirement is not the same thing as "re-creating" income for retirement. In fact, these are two completely different phases of our lives altogether. That's what you'll learn about in this guide.

Although many of today's financial advisors can assist in getting you to your envisioned "number" or help you in reaching your savings goals, not all are familiar with showing you how to convert what you have accumulated into a livable income stream that will last throughout your lifetime.

So, regardless of how much you've currently saved or where you are in the process, ask yourself this question:

Will you outlive your money, or will your money outlive you?

Turn the page, and let's get started.

STRATEGIES TO CREATE LIFETIME INCOME

ONE

Planning Means Being Prepared

If you're a baby boomer, one in the vast group of those who were born in the U.S. between 1946 and 1964, then it's likely you are quickly approaching retirement. While this is probably an exciting time for you, it can also be somewhat intimidating—especially as this is a time that can bring about a great deal of change.

In some ways, change can be good. For example, few people have an issue with *not* having to wake up early to an alarm clock every day and report to work. But, change can also fill you with worry when it comes to your expenses and how they will be paid once you leave the security of your employer's paycheck.

Throughout our working lives, we are taught how to save money for "the future." However, what we are not taught is how to take those savings and turn them into the income we will need in retirement.

That is unfortunate, too, because as retirees, while it's important to have a nice amount of savings built up, what we really need in order to live a comfortable lifestyle is *income*!

The good news is there are ways you can plan ahead for having the retirement income you'll need in the future. Just as you do with various savings and investment tools, it is important to understand there are a number of different tools that can be used for generating income, and each of these tools will have certain advantages and drawbacks, depending on what it is you are trying to accomplish.

With that in mind, being prepared for retirement and having the income you need will require you to have a good understanding of what tools are available, how each one works, and why each may—or may not—be a good fit for you and your specific retirement income goals.

Planning ahead and being better prepared can help you ensure you will have the income you require in retirement and help you reduce stress and have an overall more enjoyable retirement experience.

> *Unfortunately, many retirees are not planning ahead and do not feel better prepared for their income to last as long as they do. In fact, 25 percent of non-retirees don't have any retirement savings, and less than 40 percent of non-retirees felt prepared enough to say they felt on track with their retirement funds.[4]*

---

[4] Board of Governors of the Federal Reserve System. May 2020. "Report on the Economic Well-Being of U.S. Households in 2019, Featuring Supplemental Data from April 2020."
https://www.federalreserve.gov/publications/files/2019-report-economic-well-being-us-households-202005.pdf.

TWO

Where Are You On the Mountain?

For most of us, saving for retirement is the ultimate goal. We think, if we can just get to a particular "number" or a certain amount of money saved, then we will have made it to the "Finish Line," and all our hard work will be done.

Many of us may use several different methods of saving for retirement. For example, we might have access to an employer-sponsored retirement savings plan. In the past, many employers offered defined-benefit pension plans to their employees.

A defined-benefit pension plan—often referred to simply as a pension—provided an employee with a set amount of income guaranteed by the company when they retired. Often, the person could count on this income to come in for the remainder of his or her life.

> *There are usually two options for those who participate in defined-benefit pension plans: a lump sum or lifetime income payments. Depending on your situation, one might be more ideal for you than the other.*[5]

In the past, this pension income, coupled with what was received from Social Security retirement benefits, was often more than enough to cover what retirees needed throughout their retirement.

When a defined-benefit pension plan covered a person, the responsibility for ensuring retirement income (ensuring it would be received month in and month out, year in and year out) was up to the employer—not the employee.

This was the case regardless of what occurred in the market or even in the overall economy. If there was a shortfall in the employer's account, the funds to pay the retirement income benefits would be taken from the company's earnings.

---

[5] Roger A. Young. Kiplinger. November 19, 2019. "Should I Accept a Lump-Sum Pension Offer from My Old Employer?" https://www.kiplinger.com/article/retirement/t037-c032-s014-should-i-accept-a-lump-sum-pension-offer.html.

Throughout the years, due in large part to the expense of keeping these types of plans in force, many employers have done away with defined-benefit pension plans and have replaced them with defined-contribution plans. The most popular of these is known as the 401(k).

With a defined-contribution retirement plan, you are allowed to make tax-deferred contributions—up to a certain maximum amount—each year. In addition, if you participate in this type of plan, your employer may also contribute. Employers usually contribute in the form of matching funds, up to a certain percent of your contributions.

> *Just a few years ago, 58 million Americans participated in a 401(k) defined-contribution plan, showing just how much pensions are declining and 401(k)s are increasing in popularity.*[6]

The funds in your defined contribution retirement plan are allowed to grow on a tax-deferred basis. This means they can grow and compound without

---

[6] Investment Company Institute. June 2020. "Frequently Asked Questions About 401(k) Plan Research." https://www.ici.org/faqs/faq/401k/faqs_401k.

being taxed each year. Rather, the funds in these accounts will be taxed upon withdrawal.

If you are self-employed or work for a small business employer, you may contribute toward your retirement through various plans, including:

- SEP IRA

    A simplified employee pension (SEP) plan is an IRA that can be established by small businesses or the self-employed. They often have higher contribution limits than standard IRAs, making them more attractive in some situations. These are often created under the employee's name. As such, they allow
    an individual to contribute to a traditional IRA account.

- SIMPLE IRA

    A SIMPLE IRA is also for small-business employers and their employees. SIMPLE stands for Savings Incentive Match Plan for Employees, and it can be helpful for smaller businesses to incorporate something similar to a 401(k) plan. Employees can choose to save in these vehicles, and the employer is required to contribute, possibly via a match or other means. These also come with simpler and lower administration costs [than a traditional 401(k)] and lower contribution limits.

- SARSEP

    A SARSEP is a SEP IRA that was set up before 1997, where the IRA is funded via a salary reduction from the employees, called a "salary reduction arrangement." Many of the rules are similar to the SEP IRA since it's just a modified version of one.

- SOLO 401(k)

    The Solo 401(k) is a traditional 401(k) set up exclusively by and for a self-employed person as the sole employee of their company. It can accept individual contributions from the participant as an employee, as well as a match from the participant as their own employer. This means the individual can contribute more money to the account since there is no employer to pay the other half, allowing for a higher contribution limit.

In addition, you may also add to your retirement savings with personal savings or investment accounts. For example, you may have a bank savings account. You may also have personal investments such as stocks, bonds, or mutual funds.

You may also have a traditional or Roth IRA (individual retirement account) account. Each of these types of accounts can provide you with some nice advantages when it comes to saving for retirement.

With a traditional IRA, you may be able to deduct some or all of the money you contribute into the account. Your funds are allowed to grow on a tax-deferred basis, meaning there is no tax due until the time of withdrawal.

You can withdraw funds from your Traditional IRA anytime after you reach age fifty-nine-and-one-half without incurring a 10 percent "early withdrawal" penalty from the IRS. When you do start taking your withdrawals, the funds will be taxed at your ordinary income tax rate.

With a Traditional IRA, as with other qualified retirement plans like 401(k)s, you must start to withdraw at least some amount of money when you reach age seventy-two. Otherwise, you can be penalized. Contributions to the account can continue to be made if you still have earned income.

If your income falls within certain levels each year, you may be able to contribute to a Roth IRA. While the funds that go into a Roth IRA are after-tax dollars, the withdrawals you take from these accounts are tax-free at retirement once you are at least age fifty-nine-and-one-half and the account has been open for five years or more.

Unlike a traditional IRA, you are not *required* to begin making withdrawals from your Roth IRA at any point.

In addition to saving for the future through banks and investment companies, you may also have money in other areas, such as in real estate, collectibles, or art. There is any number of ways in which you may be saving and accumulating for your financial future.

> *In a 2019 survey, 69 percent of individuals reported they had less than $1,000 in a savings account, which increased 11 percent from the year before.*[7]

But the truth is, the actual *saving* for retirement is really just the beginning . . .

---

[7] Cameron Huddleston. GoBankingRates. December 16, 2019. "Survey: 69% of Americans Have Less Than $1,000 in Savings." https://www.gobankingrates.com/saving-money/savings-advice/americans-have-less-than-1000-in-savings/.

THREE

Accumulation vs. Distribution

While there are many ways to save and accumulate assets for our future retirement, this is just the beginning—and it is just one of the two key parts of the overall retirement picture. This first part, where we save for the future, is referred to as the accumulation phase.

In many ways, accumulation is like climbing up the "retirement mountain." During this time—which, for most of us, encompasses the majority of our working lives—we are focused on accumulating as many assets as we can and growing our nest egg for retirement.

> *It's important to start growing your nest egg early in the accumulation phase. For compound interest to have much of an effect, money needs to be invested for nearly thirty years to achieve a desired exponential outcome.*[8]

Throughout these years, we work to achieve the best return on our investments so our money will grow while, at the same time, we seek to protect principal so we don't lose what we have worked so hard to save.

During this time, we may also emphasize properly allocating assets and getting as much money as we can into these vehicles. Over time, asset allocation will usually change, especially as we move closer to retirement.

But, once we actually reach the summit of the mountain—in other words, on the day we reach retirement, and we must convert our savings into an income stream—everything begins to change. This

---

[8] Garrett Gunderson. Forbes. June 8, 2019. "Compound Interest-The Real Wealth Killer."
https://www.forbes.com/sites/garrettgunderson/2019/06/08/compound-interest-the-real-wealth-killer/#2e2a0ead2053.

is because we must now start to focus on the "other" side of the mountain—the descent.

At this time, we are now in what is referred to as the distribution phase—during this time, the financial challenges you face will be quite different from those in the accumulation phase.

For example, the focus now isn't so much on growing your nest egg but rather on preserving your capital and ensuring you have enough income to last throughout your retirement years.

You will also have different types of decisions to make during the distribution phase. For instance, you will need to determine how to best manage various concerns such as healthcare, longevity, and Social Security and how to best maintain long-term purchasing power over time. You will also need to think about how—or if—you will be able to leave anything for your loved ones going forward.

The Right Distribution Plan Makes a Difference

Regardless of the methods you use to build your savings, it is essential to have the proper income methods in place that will work for you and your specific needs in retirement. Let's take a look at an example of two investors. We will examine their investment performance over a span of years, and we will apply withdrawals to that performance to examine the distribution phase effects.

Take Jim, for example. Jim has $250,000 invested in a fund that tracks the S&P 500's returns. From 1999 to 2020, his account value grows or depletes with the market. As the table shows, Jim's portfolio takes three years of hits right at the beginning. If Jim were to begin withdrawing money as income for retirement starting in 1999, he would likely run out of money less than fifteen years into retirement.

In comparison, let's see what Jill's portfolio looks like. Jill starts with the same amount as Jim, but the returns are reversed this time, starting in 2019 and ending in 1999. By 2020, Jill's total is $200,000 more than Jim's. Because of this, if Jill were to start taking withdrawals at the beginning of the twenty-year span with inverted returns (1999 means 2019 returns, etc.), she would likely survive at least two decades into retirement, barely losing any principal. (These are hypothetical examples only, are not guaranteed, and do not reflect taxes or investment fees that would reduce the figures shown here).

Jim

Year	Beginning Value	Annual Index Return	Account Value Change	Annual Withdrawal
\$250,000 invested in S&P 500-like fund, December 1999 to December 2020, with 5% annual withdrawal increased 3% per year to address inflation			
1999	\$250,000	-10.14%	-\$25,350	\$12,500
2000	\$212,150	-13.03%	-\$27,643	\$12,875
2001	\$171,632	-23.34%	-\$40,059	\$13,261
2002	\$118,312	26.36%	\$31,187	\$13,659
2003	\$135,840	8.99%	\$12,212	\$14,069
2004	\$133,983	2.97%	\$3,979	\$14,491
2005	\$123,471	13.62%	\$16,817	\$14,926
2006	\$125,362	3.53%	\$4,425	\$15,373
2007	\$114,414	-38.49%	-\$44,038	\$15,835
2008	\$54,541	23.48%	\$12,806	\$16,310
2009	\$51,038	12.83%	\$6,548	\$16,799
2010	\$40,787	0.00%	\$0	\$17,303
2011	\$23,484	13.35%	\$3,135	\$17,822
2012	\$8,798	29.59%	\$2,603	\$18,357
2013	-\$6,956	11.36%	-\$790	\$18,907
2014	-\$26,653	-0.73%	\$195	\$19,475
2015	-\$45,933	9.54%	-\$4,382	\$20,059
2016	-\$70,374	19.44%	-\$13,681	\$20,661
2017	-\$104,716	-6.25%	\$6,545	\$21,280
2018	-\$119,451	6.59%	-\$7,872	\$21,919
2019	-\$149,242	30.43%	-\$45,414	\$22,576
2020	-\$217,233			

Jill

$250,000 invested in S&P 500-like fund, December 1999 to December 2020, with 5% annual withdrawal increased 3% per year to address inflation

Year	Beginning Value	Annual Index Return	Account Value Change	Annual Withdrawal
2019	$250,000	30.43%	$76,075	$12,500
2018	$313,575	6.59%	$20,665	$12,875
2017	$321,365	-6.25%	-$20,085	$13,261
2016	$288,018	19.44%	$55,991	$13,659
2015	$330,350	9.54%	$31,515	$14,069
2014	$347,796	-0.73%	-$2,539	$14,491
2013	$330,766	11.36%	$37,575	$14,926
2012	$353,416	29.59%	$104,576	$15,373
2011	$442,618	13.35%	$59,090	$15,835
2010	$485,873	0.00%	$0	$16,310
2009	$469,563	12.83%	$60,245	$16,799
2008	$513,009	23.48%	$120,455	$17,303
2007	$616,161	-38.49%	-$237,160	$17,822
2006	$361,179	3.53%	$12,750	$18,357
2005	$355,572	13.62%	$48,429	$18,907
2004	$385,093	2.97%	$11,437	$19,475
2003	$377,056	8.99%	$33,897	$20,059
2002	$390,894	26.36%	$103,040	$20,661
2001	$473,273	-23.34%	-$110,462	$21,280
2000	$341,531	-13.03%	-$44,501	$21,919
1999	$275,111	-10.14%	-$27,896	$22,576
2020	$224,638			

So, how can this be?

It is because Jim suffered a large loss in the initial years while Jill did not experience the same loss percentage until a later time in the phase.

Therefore, even with the same returns in the distribution phase for both investors, when they are both drawing income from the portfolio, the fact Jim suffered a loss earlier in the time frame made a significant difference.

What exactly does this tell us?

One of the key points is we need to know and understand the inherent risks threatening the distribution phase. This is because, while during the accumulation phase your *average* return may still allow you to come out with a positive number at the end of a certain time period, the same may *not* hold true when you are taking withdrawals from your portfolio.

> *Unlike Jim and Jill, 40 percent of American retirees don't even have any personal savings and rely solely on the government's provision of Social Security benefits as their only income.*[9]

Do You Have the Right Type of Guide?

Unfortunately, many of the financial advisors who work with investors on helping them to grow their assets during their accumulation phase are not familiar with the challenges retirees will face—or the solutions they will require—once they reach the distribution stage.

That is why working with an income planning professional for the second phase of your life is often a desirable option. While retirement can bring about joy for many people, it can also be scary not knowing where your income will come from once

---

[9] Will Englund. *The Washington Post*. May 4, 2020.
"Millions of baby boomers are getting caught in the country's broken retirement system."
https://www.washingtonpost.com/business/2020/05/04/baby-boomers-retirement/.

you leave your employer. On top of that, many people face the very real possibility that one day they could run out of money.

> *Because of the COVID-19 pandemic in 2020, half of Americans who responded to one study claimed they would run out of money in the month of April. If many people who aren't in retirement are running out of money, how many people in retirement must be struggling to keep afloat?*[10]

An income planning professional can help you to sort out what you have, what you will need, and ways to proceed in order to accomplish your retirement income goals so you don't need to spend your "golden years" living in constant financial fear.

---

[10] Maurie Backman. The Motley Fool. April 10, 2020. "50% of Americans Say Their Savings Will Run Out This Month." https://www.fool.com/retirement/2020/04/10/50-of-americans-say-their-savings-will-run-out-thi.aspx.

> *Even now, according to one study, 61 percent of Americans don't know how much money they will need to avoid running out of money in retirement. This is why an income plan is beneficial and reassuring.[11]*

By having a clear-cut plan, you will be able to re-create a retirement "paycheck" for yourself, so you will have a regular income you can count on for paying your living expenses, as well as for your travel and fun.

Going forward without an income plan is like trying to navigate down an icy mountainside without the help of ropes, picks, or a map. It can be extremely difficult—and detrimental—to your financial situation.

An income planner can create a retirement income "map" designed for you and your personal needs, goals, and time horizon, taking into consideration how much you currently have saved, how much longer you plan to work, and any other specifics

---

[11] Rebecca Lake. Investopedia. August 6, 2019. "Retirement Planning Doesn't Stop When You Retire." https://www.investopedia.com/retirement/retirement-planning-doesnt-stop-when-you-retire/.

you may have. And, the sooner you start, the sooner you will have your step-by-step guide in place that can put you on the path to your income desires.

FOUR

Avoid Common Income Planning Mistakes

Although retirement can be an exciting time in your life, one of the most daunting things retirees face is managing their personal finances. This is because from the moment you leave the "security" of a steady paycheck from your employer, you must now rely on other financial sources to sustain you throughout the remainder of your life.

These sources will typically include income from Social Security, as well as income from any personal savings and/or retirement accounts you may have participated in throughout the years. In order to ensure you will have enough income to pay your ongoing living expenses, as well as enough to sustain you for an unknown period of time (i.e., the remainder of your lifetime), it will require you to set up a plan.

That income plan you create will need to include the right tools for the job—these financial tools will typically differ from those you used for saving and growing your wealth throughout your accumulation phase.

Are You Using the Right Tools?

Using the right tools going forward will entail asking and answering some important questions. Some of these questions may be difficult or uncomfortable to deal with, but they are essential in the overall process of creating your future income plan.

A good way to start is getting an estimate of what your living expenses will be when you retire. This will help you to come up with an approximate monthly income that will be required (don't forget to allocate for emergencies).

> *When planning for retirement, most pre-retirees underestimate their living costs in retirement by assuming they will only spend 70 or 80 percent of what they currently spend before retirement. Due to inflation and other factors, this assumption often proves unrealistic.*[12]

You should also consider additional questions because the unexpected can—and sometimes does—occur. Planning for this is key in either being well prepared or falling into financial hardship.

For instance, your future income plan should accommodate for situations such as:

- What if you died tomorrow?

- Would your spouse have enough income to live comfortably?

---

[12] Arthur Pinkasovitch. Investopedia. November 14, 2019. "These five steps will help you toward a safe, secure, and fun retirement." https://www.investopedia.com/articles/retirement/11/5-steps-to-retirement-plan.asp#2-determine-retirement-spending-needs.

- How much of your estate or assets will be subject to taxation?

- What if your spouse died tomorrow?

- Would your income and lifestyle be affected?

- Would your Social Security or pension income be eliminated or reduced?

- What if your pension check were to be reduced by 10 to 20 percent next year?

- What if inflation grew more rapidly than anticipated over the next ten to twenty years?

- What if you or your spouse needed long-term care?

- What if the stock market fell by 50 percent over the next two years?

- What if you or your spouse lived to be 100 years old? Would your income last that long?

> *According to the Transamerica Center for Retirement Studies, over one-fifth of Baby Boomers are expected to live until the age range of ninety to ninety-nine, and another one-tenth are expected to live past the age of one hundred.*[13]

Many financial advisors focus only on having their clients go "up" the mountain during the accumulation phase. They strive to use the best tools they can find for their clients, based on the clients' specific needs, risk tolerance, and goals.

But, as you get closer to retirement—and certainly as you reach the "summit" of the retirement mountain—the tools you need to use in order to get you safely where you need to go will likely change dramatically.

Another way to think about it is to imagine if financial tools were like household tools in a toolbox. If you needed to hang a picture on the wall, would you use a hammer or a screwdriver to pound a nail into that wall?

---

[13] Michael Keenan. GoBankingRates. April 6, 2020. "31 Surprising Facts About Retiring You Probably Didn't Know." https://www.gobankingrates.com/retirement/planning/weird-things-about-retiring/.

Hopefully, most people would use the hammer!

Even though the screwdriver is a perfectly good tool, it is efficient for *other uses*—not for the job at hand. Financial tools, just like any other type of tool, when used in a manner they were not specifically designed for, will often not be able to effectively or efficiently perform the task.

> *Over a third of older Americans rely solely on Social Security benefits for income even when the Social Security Administration advises benefits should only account for 40 percent of low-earners full retirement age income.*[14]

Both before and after retiring, some of the most common mistakes people make with their finances can include:

- Trying to make a financial tool do something it was not designed to do. (For

---

[14] Frank Porell and Tyler Bond. National Institute of Retirement Security. January 2020. "Examining the Nest Egg: The Sources of Retirement Income for Older Americans."; https://www.nirsonline.org/reports/examining-the-nest-egg/ Social Security Administration. 2020. "Understanding the Benefits." https://www.ssa.gov/pubs/EN-05-10024.pdf.

example, many of the investments you have used to save and grow your wealth may not be the same "tools" you will need to provide ongoing retirement income.)

- Using too few tools (i.e., not diversifying enough or "having all of your eggs in just one basket." This can be risky because, if there is a market correction, a large percentage of assets could be lost at a time when it may be difficult—or even impossible—to recoup them).

- Not realizing there could be a better tool to do a particular job. (Many of the financial professionals who help us save and invest during the accumulation phase of life are not familiar with the challenges retirees face or the financial tools needed for producing ongoing retirement income. Therefore, it may be necessary to work with a professional who focuses specifically in the income planning area in order to obtain better guidance.)

> *A quality financial income planner will hold extensive knowledge of taxes, Social Security, and other financial products useful for creating income payments in retirement—such knowledge will often take years of experience and training to accumulate.*

FIVE

Recreating a Paycheck

There are many different ways to go about recreating a paycheck. Depending on your specific situation, needs, and goals, what you use for your income in retirement may differ a great deal from what someone else uses. In other words, there is no single best way to create income in retirement that works ideally for everyone.

While the most important step in ensuring you have enough retirement income is having an income plan, there are different financial tools you might use that can essentially help you with re-creating a paycheck.

These financial vehicles, in one way or another, provide income either on a regular or a sporadic basis and can be used for paying for living expenses or other needs in retirement. Each may have various advantages and drawbacks, depending on your specific needs. Let's take a closer look at these income-producing tools.

Social Security

While there has been much debate over the years about whether or not Social Security will be around to pay out benefits to baby boomers in the future, the truth is this program will likely be a part of your overall retirement income plan—provided you have enough work credits and you qualify for benefits. The key is not to count on Social Security for *all* of your retirement income needs.

> *Even if the Social Security's trust funds are completely depleted (currently projected to happen in 2035), benefits will not stop altogether. Unless Congress steps in to make changes, baby boomers face only a 20 percent reduction in benefits, not a 100 percent loss.*[15]

---

[15] Maurie Backman. The Motley Fool. January 28, 2020. "Is Social Security Really Running Out of Money?" https://www.fool.com/retirement/2020/01/28/is-social-security-really-running-out-of-money.aspx.

That is because, according to the Social Security Administration itself, "Social Security was never meant to be the only source of income for people when they retire. Social Security replaces about 40 percent of an average wage earner's income after retiring . . ."[16]

> *In order to qualify for Social Security benefits, the average person needs a total of forty credits. Each person earns a credit when they make $1,470 (in 2021) and can earn up to four credits a year.*[17]

What many people don't know is there are ways of maximizing their Social Security income just by taking advantage of how and when they claim benefits. In some cases, this can make a difference of $50,000 or even $100,000 in total benefits received throughout a lifetime.

Not all financial planners are aware of the ins and outs of how Social Security retirement income

---

[16] Social Security. 2020. "Understanding the Benefits." https://www.ssa.gov/pubs/EN-05-10024.pdf.

[17] Social Security Administration. 2021. "Understanding the Benefits." https://www.ssa.gov/pubs/EN-05-10024.pdf.

works. This is why working with someone who is a professional income planner is so important.

> *Depending on when you were born, full retirement age (FRA) fluctuates and determines when you can receive your full Social Security benefit. If you apply for your benefit at your designated FRA, you will receive the full benefit. If you file before FRA (as early as age sixty-two), your benefit will be diminished. If you delay filing for Social Security past your FRA, your benefit will increase by a percentage, up to the age of seventy.[18]*

Pension

If you are one of the few who work for an employer who still offers a defined-benefit pension plan, then you already certainly have one way to re-create your paycheck. Typically, a defined-benefit pension will provide you with a set amount of retirement income throughout the remainder of your life.

---

[18] Social Security Administration. 2020. "Understanding the Benefits." https://www.ssa.gov/pubs/EN-05-10024.pdf.

> *While pension payments are made for the rest of your life, many employers offer a lump sum option for employees, allowing them to accept a large sum of money instead of the monthly payments. One study even discovered that 21 percent of retirees completely drain their lump sum payment after just over five years.[19]*

If you are married, you will generally need to decide how to receive your pension distributions. In this case, there are usually two primary options. The first option includes taking a payout based upon your own life expectancy only. This will provide you with the highest dollar amount of income during your lifetime. The drawback to this particular option is the income will cease upon your death.

The second payout option is to choose a survivor benefit. Here, you will get a smaller amount of regular income. However, upon your death, your spouse will continue to receive an income stream

---

[19] Troy Segal. Investopedia. February 28, 2020. "Lump-Sum Vs. Regular Pension Payments: What's the Difference?" https://www.investopedia.com/articles/retirement/05/lumpsumpension.asp#citation-6.

from the payments you received while you were living. This can be a good choice if your spouse will be counting on your pension for a large percentage of his or her own retirement income.

> *Many pension survivor benefits allow only 50 to 75 percent of a pension paycheck to continue being paid after the employed spouse passes away. This means they do guarantee income for two lifetimes, but those income paychecks are reduced.*[20]

Annuities

Annuities are a type of insurance product. These financial vehicles are designed to accept funds—either one single lump sum or a series of premium payments over time—and then, upon "annuitization," to pay out a stream of income payments.

The annuity holder can typically choose how and how often those income payments are received.

---

[20] Women's Institue for a Secure Retirement. "Pension and Survivor Benefits."
https://www.wiserwomen.org/resources/retirement-planning-resources/pension-and-survivor-benefits/.

Usually, however, annuities will offer a lifetime income option where income is guaranteed to continue for the remainder of your life, regardless of how long you live.

> *Annuities often present a less volatile option for income than the stock market, and, in 2020, Americans were so interested in more stable income options that $58.6 billion were spent on annuity sales in just the first few months of the year.*[21]

In annuities with lifetime income options, you will typically be able to choose a second income recipient (either a spouse or a significant other, although it does not have to be either of those) to also receive income for the remainder of his or her lifetime, too.

In addition to your account value, the amount of the income payment you receive from an annuity is based on several other factors. These include:

---

[21] LIMRA. March 9, 2021. "Secure Retirement Institute: Total Annuity Sales Fall 9% in 2020."

- **Your Age:** One significant criteria contributing to the amount of annuity income payments you receive will be your age (as well as the age of the joint income recipient, if applicable). This is because age obviously plays a factor in life expectancy. The older you are when you begin your annuity income payments, the higher your income payment is likely to be. This is because the older you are, the shorter your life expectancy. The shorter your life expectancy, the shorter the amount of time the annuity will likely have to pay you income.

> *Many financial professionals recommend age seventy to seventy-five as the most ideal age for annuitizing income, since this usually allows for the highest payout.*[22]

- **Your Gender:** Gender is another key component in how the insurance company

---

[22] Richard Best. July 20, 2020. "What Is the Best Age to Get an Annuity?"
https://www.investopedia.com/articles/markets/072216/what-best-age-get-annuity.asp.

determines the amount of your annuity income payment. That is because this, too, has an effect on your life expectancy. On average, females live longer than males. Therefore, all other factors being equal, a sixty-five-year-old male with a lifetime income option is likely to receive a higher amount of income from his annuity than a sixty-five-year-old female.

- **Payout Option Selected:** The income payout option you select will also play a part in how much income you receive. This is because it will affect how long the income payments will last. For instance, you may decide to go with an income payout that only lasts for ten years for certain versus a guaranteed lifetime option. In that case, the ten-year option would pay a higher dollar amount than the lifetime income option.

- **Interest Rate:** Because the insurance company holding your annuity will be investing your funds, the amount you receive in income will also depend on the insurer's expected investment returns on your money. The amount can also depend on whether you select a fixed annuity or a variable annuity. With a fixed annuity, the amount of your income payment will not change over time. However, with a variable payout, the income amount can fluctuate based upon market conditions.

> *Fees can also counteract the expected interest rate, with the average for variable annuities without additional add-ons resting at between 3% and 4% percent in 2021.[23]*

- **Insurance Company:** The actual insurance company you select to purchase your annuity through can also be a factor in the amount of your income payment. Prior to purchasing an annuity, it will be important to check the financial strength and stability of the underlying insurer, as well as its reputation for paying out its policyholder claims.

In terms of receiving retirement income, annuities can provide you with certain advantages—especially if you opt for the lifetime income option.

---

[23] The Annuity Expert. "Annuity Fees." https://annuityexpertadvice.com/annuity-101/annuity-fees/.

This could reassure you that you—and possibly your spouse or other chosen individual—would receive a "paycheck" for the remainder of your life.

In fact, many of today's annuities can eliminate the risk of outliving your money. Even variable and fixed indexed annuities can provide assured lifetime income by offering a guaranteed withdrawal benefit, often for an additional annual fee. This can essentially shift longevity risk to the insurance company and ensure you have an income stream for the remainder of your lifetime—regardless of how long that may be.

Also, if you have purchased an annuity outside of a qualified retirement account or IRA (in other words, if you have purchased an annuity in a personal savings or investment account), then the income you receive from that annuity will only be partially taxable.

That is because a portion of that income will be considered a return of your original premium, while another portion of each income payment will be considered gain, which represents the interest you received. The portion that is considered gain will be taxable to you as ordinary income, and the portion that is considered a return of your premium will be non-taxable.

There are several factors to consider prior to purchasing an annuity. For example, there are typically surrender charges that are associated with annuities. A surrender charge is an amount you must pay during the first several years you own the annuity if you withdraw your money.

In most cases, you will be able to withdraw a certain amount—usually 10 percent of the contract value—without penalty. The amount of the surrender charge will typically decrease each year, until it eventually reaches 0 percent. For example, an annuity may have a surrender charge of 8 percent in the first year and then may drop by 1 percent each year after that for the next seven years, until there is no surrender charge remaining.

It is important to keep in mind that an annuity should be considered a long-term endeavor. Therefore, if you feel you will need the funds for other uses, then this may not be the right financial option for you.

Once you annuitize (i.e., turn your lump sum of cash into an income stream), you are essentially giving up control of these funds to the insurance company. Converting your lump sum of cash into income is an irreversible decision—so, once you have done so, there is no way to convert the money back into the savings you have built up.

Also, if you (and your spouse or other income recipient, if applicable) were to pass away within a short period of time and without receiving very much income, then (depending on how you elect to receive income from the annuity) the money would basically be gone. This is because, in many instances, the insurance company keeps the remainder of your funds when you pass away. This could have a negative effect on what your beneficiaries inherit.

> *Variable annuities allow you to receive income payments for life, enjoy tax deferrals on your gains, and provide ease in changing investments; but, on the other hand, they are subject to market risk and potential loss of principal.*[24]

On the contrary, if you were to live for a long period of time, the income you receive from the annuity may or may not be able to keep up with the rising cost of inflation. With that in mind, it is important to understand exactly how, and how

---

[24] Barclay Palmer. Investopedia. July 12, 2020. "Getting the Whole Story on Variable Annuities."
https://www.investopedia.com/retirement/variable-annuities-whole-story/.

much, income would be received in both the short and the long-term time horizon, as it could affect your retirement lifestyle.

Dividend Income

Another tool often used for receiving retirement income is dividends. Dividends are actually a distribution of a portion of a company's earnings. These may come from stocks or mutual funds you own.

Many retirees will invest in dividend-paying equities in order to take advantage of the steady payments that can be used as income. As an added bonus, there are numerous dividend-paying stocks that represent mature, financially stable companies whose stock prices also continue to rise over time.

In many cases, the dividend payment may also periodically rise, providing these retirees with an increase in income. This can help to keep pace with inflation over time, as the price of goods and services you need to purchase in the future will also likely be rising.

Although dividends are not guaranteed, they can provide you with a way to potentially generate a consistent amount of cash flow from companies that are typically less volatile than the stock market in general.

Also, unlike with purchasing an annuity, while your assets are fully invested, they are also much more liquid. This means that, in case of an emergency, you could essentially get to your money if you needed it.

There are some things to consider, though, when using a dividend income strategy. First, just as any other asset invested in the stock market, you do run the risk of volatility. Over the past several years, the stock market has been particularly unpredictable—even for stable, blue-chip equities. Therefore, it is important to be aware of your risk tolerance and the amount of your total portfolio you have invested in equities.

> *Dividend investing requires little to no fees, with most firms and companies reducing trading fees to cost nothing, and, with the introduction of fractional investing through technology, it requires very little money to invest in. Volatility, though, is the most crucial concern.*[25]

Also, the dividends you receive will typically be fully taxable to you as income. With that in mind, you will need to be aware of your net income in terms of your ability to pay living expenses in retirement.

The dividends you receive could also affect the taxability of your Social Security retirement benefits. Therefore, be sure you are aware of how this—and any other income strategy you choose—could affect your other retirement benefits.

---

[25] Dividend Diplomats. July 17, 2020. "5 Reasons Dividend Income is the Easiest Passive Income Source." https://www.dividenddiplomats.com/easiest-passive-income-source/.

Interest-Only Withdrawals

In order to reduce market risk, some retirees opt to purchase protected financial vehicles such as bonds and/or CDs (certificates of deposit) and use the interest from these investments as income. With this strategy, you can essentially protect your principal from downturns in the market.

Yet, while this may seem like a relatively secure option because you aren't "losing" money in the market, there are actually some real, inherent risks. For one, you can lose future purchasing power by not being able to keep pace with inflation. This can be just as detrimental as market volatility—if not more.

Over time, inflation can play a key role in affecting retirement income. And, because people on average live so much longer these days, it is essential to factor in the protection of future purchasing power into your retirement income plan.

> *While they don't always keep pace with inflation, both bonds and CDs are helpful in balancing out a diverse portfolio because of how they protect principal.*[26]

As an example, using an average inflation rate of just 3.22 percent, prices double approximately every twenty years. Therefore, your future purchasing power could be cut in half in just a twenty-year period of time. This means, twenty years from now, you would need to generate double the amount of income you are creating today to buy the very same goods and services to lead essentially the same lifestyle.

Said another way, if you were to retire today and your fixed investments were generating $4,000 per month for you, then, in twenty years, with inflation at 3.22 percent, you would need to be generating $8,000 per month to maintain the same lifestyle you enjoy now.

There can be other risks with this income option, too—especially if you are locking your money

---

[26] Dayana Yochim. NerdWallet. August 15, 2019. "The Best Investments You Can Make Right Now." https://www.nerdwallet.com/blog/investing/the-best-investments-right-now/.

away for longer periods of time to take advantage of higher interest rates. This can come in the form of reinvestment risk—not being able to find comparable yields due to a changing interest rate environment. In fact, you could essentially lose out on other investment or income opportunities, too, by having large sums of money locked away for long periods of time at low rates.

The yields, or interest rates, on bonds are not always guaranteed. Therefore, the amount of income you receive won't necessarily be guaranteed, depending on the type of bond you purchase and can fluctuate. There can also be an inverse relationship between interest rates and the value of the bond itself.

So, if you do need to sell the bond early (prior to its maturity date) for one reason or another, you could end up netting less than what you paid for it. Likewise, a change in the quality of the bond can also affect its value and the amount of the income you receive.

In addition, the income received from the interest on bonds, as well as CDs, will most often be fully taxable as ordinary income. Because of this, there is the possibility it could affect the taxability of your Social Security retirement benefits, too.

> *You pay tax on 85 percent of your Social Security benefit if your combined income falls above $34,000 as an individual and $44,000 filing jointly.*[27]

Liquidate Assets

In some cases, it makes sense to liquidate a portion of your assets as you need retirement income. Depending on your specific needs, this may mean selling off 2 or 3 percent of your total portfolio each year while allowing the remainder of your assets to continue to grow.

This strategy allows you to maintain control over your portfolio. It also gives you the ability to alter your plans over time should your needs change. In addition, if your portfolio experiences significant growth during a particular period of time, you could essentially take out a larger amount of income. The alternative is, if there should be a market downturn, you could end up with some periods where you have less income, too.

---

[27] Social Security Administration. 2020. "Income Taxes And Your Social Security Benefit."
https://www.ssa.gov/benefits/retirement/planner/taxes.html.

There is a fair amount of risk involved when using this strategy, given such a large percentage of your assets are invested in the market. However, depending on how much you have left at your passing, you may end up being able to provide your beneficiaries with a significant inheritance.

It will be important to keep in mind how—and how much—you will be taxed when liquidating various assets. This is because the taxation can differ depending on whether the account is qualified versus non-qualified and whether the money you are withdrawing from the portfolio is interest or a capital gain—and, even further, whether a capital gain was short or long-term.

There is also another inherent risk involved when using this strategy many people aren't fully aware of but need to be. That is something known as "order of returns risk." While many of us are familiar with how the market can produce both positive and negative returns over time, we don't necessarily always pay attention to the sequence of each year's return. But this can make a big difference in how long your money lasts throughout your life. This is especially the case with returns that occur as you near retirement.

A negative return in your portfolio just before you start to take withdrawals can have a substantial long-term negative effect going forward, essentially causing you to run out of money faster—and in some cases, *much* faster, just like our earlier example of the two investors, Jim and Jill.

Remember the example in section three? The two investors had the exact same returns, but the difference in their portfolios' longevity when the investors began taking income withdrawals was greatly affected by the order of the returns. Having negative returns earlier on can affect your portfolio's ability to generate income much more than negative returns later in retirement.

Those who retired on portfolios depleted in the market downturns of the early and late 2000s experienced much more instability than those who saw those downturns after having had the upswings of the nineties and mid-2000s.

> *One way to minimize the "order of return risk" is to keep five to ten years' worth of income protected in a place where the market can't touch it. This allows you to avoid the adverse effects of a down market in your first few years of retirement.*[28]

With that in mind, once you begin to take withdrawals from your portfolio—and even as you approach that time in your life—it is important to be mindful of not just the returns on your portfolio, but also the *order* of when those returns occur.

This is particularly essential today, as people are living so much longer, and, in most cases, income will be required for many years in retirement. Remember, longevity is the intensifier of all other financial risks.

---

[28] T. Eric Reich. Kiplinger. Jan. 3, 2020. "Retirees Can't Afford to Underestimate Sequence of Return Risk." https://www.kiplinger.com/article/retirement/t037-c032-s014-retirees-can-t-overlook-sequence-of-return-risk.html.

The Time-Based Segmentation System

You may also consider an income strategy known as "The Time-Based Segmentation System." This system works by allocating certain portions of money to be used at different times for specific needs. These may be for income purposes or other goals related to financial planning and estate planning.

While all of the other income strategies discussed above have various advantages and drawbacks, the time-based segmentation system has taken these and attempted to gain the maximum amount of advantages while at the same time eliminating the most drawbacks.

For example, this method keeps your assets well-diversified. While this approach can't ensure a profit or ensure you won't lose money, by not being too heavily weighted in just one area, your risk is diminished, which can help you preserve your principal for a longer period of time.

Because certain guarantees can be built into the model, with the time-based segmentation system, you always know where your next "paycheck" is coming from. This provides you with a level of certainty your living expenses will be covered in retirement.

It can also help protect you against two of the biggest risks many retirees face—the high cost of a long-term care need and the substantial cost of an estate tax liability. Take long-term care, for instance. According to Genworth's Cost of Care Survey, the national median daily rate for a private room in a skilled nursing home in 2020 was $290.[29]

That equals more than $100,000 per year!

How long would it take most people to deplete their entire retirement portfolio with that amount of expense? And, receiving care in your home—where most people would rather be—is also very costly.

Based on the same Genworth study, the national median hourly rate for both homemaker services and for home health aide services was about $24. So, even if you needed someone to help you or a loved one for just a few hours each day, the amount could really add up.

---

[29] Genworth.com. 2020. "Genworth 2021 Cost of Care Survey." https://www.genworth.com/aging-and-you/finances/cost-of-care.html.

> *In short, a time-based segmentation system divides funds into time segments to keep a withdrawal rate that matches the time left after retirement. When referring to more than just time-based segments, this strategy can also be called a "bucket strategy."*[30]

Having a method for protecting you from this type of financial risk is essential—as is protecting for the potential payment of an estate tax liability. In 2021, there are twelve different estate tax "brackets." These range from 18 percent to 40 percent.[31]

Following are the current rates and the estate sizes they apply to for 2021.

---

[30] Justin Kuepper. Investopedia. August 15, 2019. "Bucket Strategy vs. Systematic Withdrawals: Knowing the Difference." https://www.investopedia.com/articles/financial-advisors/060815/comparison-bucket-strategy-vs-systematic-withdrawals.asp.

[31] Amelia Josephson. smartasset.com. Jan. 22, 2021. "A Guide to the Federal Estate Tax for 2021" https://smartasset.com/taxes/all-about-the-estate-tax.

Estate Tax Rates 2021

For Taxable Estates Between...	And...	You'll Pay This Amount of Tax...	Plus, You'll Pay __ on the Amount in Excess of the Lower Limit
$0	$10,000	$0	18%
$10,001	$20,000	$1,800	20%
$20,001	$40,000	$3,800	22%
$40,001	$60,000	$8,200	24%
$60,001	$80,000	$13,000	26%
$80,001	$100,000	$18,200	28%
$100,001	$150,000	$23,800	30%
$150,001	$250,000	$38,800	32%
$250,001	$500,000	$70,800	34%
$500,001	$750,000	$155,800	37%
$750,001	$1,000,000	$248,300	39%
$1,000,001	-----------	$345,800	40%

But, before you get too nervous about having to pay estate taxes, this chart only tells part of the story. This is because there is a lifetime exemption allowed. In other words, there is an amount you are allowed to give your heirs that is excluded from estate taxation. In 2021, this amount is $11.7 million.[32] This means many estates in the U.S. are not subject to estate taxes at all.

In addition to the lifetime exclusion, there is also an annual gift tax exemption that allows you to give a certain amount away to as many people as you wish, each and every year. In 2021, the maximum amount you can gift to each person is $15,000. As a married couple, you can gift up to $30,000 to as many people as you wish—$15,000 from each spouse.

With the time-based segmentation system, you can pass on more of your legacy to your heirs in a tax-efficient and effective manner. This strategy may also provide you with additional advantages as well, such as reducing the risk you will outlive your money due to a longer retirement time frame. And, it may also provide you with a rising amount of income over time in order to keep pace with the increasing future costs of goods and services.

As with any of the other income strategies, though, it will be important to ensure that, based on your

---

[32] Ibid.

specific circumstances, you do not take on too much market risk or, conversely, expose yourself to too much reinvestment risk, depending on which financial tools you select.

The Bottom Line on Recreating a Paycheck

Retirement can be the best years of your life, or it can be a period of years spent struggling just to get by. It all depends on how—and how well—you are able to create a livable income stream to meet your needs.

Prior to leaving the security of an employer's income, it will be necessary to "re-create" a paycheck you can count on in retirement. And, because people are living so much longer today, that paycheck will ideally be able to last for many years, or possibly even be *guaranteed* to last for the remainder of your lifetime, regardless of how long that may be.

> *In 2020, 55 million Americans were aged sixty-five and older, and that number is growing, with 95 million people projected to be in this category by 2060. With so many people getting older, it's important to consider what life in retirement could look like for you and your loved ones.[33]*

There are many strategies available for re-creating a paycheck. Each will have certain advantages and drawbacks, depending on your goals, risk tolerance, time horizon, and other financial requirements.

In some cases, just one income method may suffice, and, in others, a combination of strategies may work best for fulfilling your needs while avoiding certain types of risk. What may work for one investor or retiree may not be best for another.

With that in mind, it is always best to weigh all of the potential pros and cons of any financial strategy you are considering, as well as the possible consequences for both the short and long-term time horizon. You may also wish to discuss these with your tax advisor or CPA before moving forward.

---

[33] Julia Kagan. Investopedia. Jan. 18, 2020. "Longevity Risk." https://www.investopedia.com/terms/l/longevityrisk.asp.

SIX

Case Study Retirement
Income Planning with Your
Specific Objectives in Mind

With so many different financial tools available in the marketplace, it can be difficult to sort through them all. In addition, there is no particular retirement savings or income plan that is right for everyone across the board.

In fact, there can be a wide array of factors that make one strategy ideal for some people and a bad idea for others. There are a number of criteria that need to be analyzed before designing a plan that fits with your specific objectives, including your:

- Current age
- Marital status
- Time frame until retirement
- Risk tolerance

- Amount saved
- Estimated expenses and income needs in retirement
- Other retirement income sources (such as Social Security and/or an employer-sponsored pension plan)
- Taxable versus tax-free retirement income generators
- Anticipated life expectancy
- Estimated healthcare and/or long-term care costs
- Legacy intentions

So, creating a customized retirement income plan requires a good understanding of how different financial vehicles work and whether they will be a good fit for accomplishing your objectives.

Further, there is a big difference between having an unrelated mix of investments in your portfolio versus creating an actual income plan where all of the financial tools correlate with one another.

These financial "cogs" in the wheel must also be timed appropriately. That's because if you retire (i.e., start generating income from your portfolio) too early, you run the risk of depleting your assets while they are still needed. On the other hand, if you wait "too long," you could end up robbing yourself of days that could have been spent doing things you enjoy with people you love and care about.

Take, for instance, William and Mary Richmond (a hypothetical couple). When they were sixty-four and sixty-two, respectively, the couple was unsure of when they would be able to retire (although ideally, they would like to do so in three years, when Mary turns sixty-five). Married for thirty-four years, William and Mary have three adult children who are all self-sufficient.

They were both well-established in their careers—Mary as a nurse and William as an electrical engineer. Together, they brought in over $200,000 per year. One of their biggest concerns is being able to "replace" their paychecks with retirement income generated from several different sources, including:

- Social Security
- Employer-sponsored pensions
- Defined contribution plans (in this case, a 401(k) and a 403(b))

Ideally, William and Mary planned to downsize their home when they retired—which will save them money on property taxes each year—and moved closer to the beach and to their grandchildren. Although they had been regularly saving over the past few decades, the couple was unsure of how to maximize their income from Social Security.

They were also unclear on how to convert their savings into an ongoing retirement income stream that will last for as long as they need it to—especially if the stock market experienced a correction.

Not wanting to make any decisions that could negatively impact their financial future, William and Mary decided to meet with a retirement income planning professional. In order to make the best recommendations for the couple, the advisor asks William and Mary a series of questions.

This allows the advisor to determine a "starting point" (where William and Mary are financially right now), as well as to get a better idea of what the couple's ideal retirement would look like. Making any recommendations without first having this knowledge could risk putting the wrong financial tools in place which, in turn, would put William and Mary at risk of not accomplishing their goals.

The Planning Process

In order to address all of the concerns that the Richmonds had, the advisor focused on five key areas. These covered all of the "bases" for a comprehensive, well-thought-out retirement income plan. They included:

1. Income Planning
2. Investment Management
3. Tax Planning
4. Healthcare Planning and Wellness
5. Legacy and Estate Management

He then took a closer look at each of these by focusing on key areas in each section as follows:

Income Planning

Many retirees generate income from more than just one single source—and not all of them start at the same time. That's why it is essential to analyze anticipated expenses along with income amounts, and to then make sure that there is enough coming in to cover living expenses, and ideally non-essentials like entertainment and fun.

The three primary income sources for retirees can include:

- Employer pension
- Social Security
- Interest / Dividends / Portfolio Drawdowns from Personal Savings and Investments

Because people are living longer (on average) today, factoring inflation into the plan is extremely important so that retirees can still continue to purchase the items and services that they need. So, the income advisor includes this into the plan for William and Mary.

With an average inflation rate of just 3.2%, income would need to double in twenty years in order to just keep pace with their current lifestyle today. The couple's current monthly expenses are approximately $4,500, not including one-time purchases. These monthly costs are categorized as follows:

Monthly Expenses
William and Mary Richmond

Auto and Transport	$342	Bills and Utilities	$1,003
Business	$0	Charitable Giving	$100
Dining Out	$150	Education	$0
Entertainment	$500	Fees and Charges	$85
Gifts	$100	Groceries	$750
Health and Fitness	$250	Kids	$200
Miscellaneous	$250	Shopping	$350
Travel	$325	Other	$195

There are also several one-time purchases that the couple incurs each year, such as:

- Mortgage (until it is paid off)
- Taxes
- Homeowner's Insurance
- Car Payment (until it is paid off)
- Healthcare
- Other

Altogether, when divided out on a per-month basis, William and Mary's monthly expenses equal $7,586. This is the figure that the retirement income planner uses for the couple's estimated monthly outgo in their first year of retirement.

One of the primary income sources that William and Mary would be able to count on is Social Security. William's monthly benefit at his full retirement age of sixty-six is $2,764, while Mary's income would be $2,193 per month at her FRA of sixty-six and four months.

Because Social Security can be claimed as early as age sixty-two—at a reduced dollar amount—the couple has several different claiming options to choose from, including:

Mary's Age	Amount (PIA)
62	$1,645
63	$1,754
64	$1,940
65	$2,083
66 FRA	$2,193
67	$2,368
68	$2.543
69	$2,719
70	$2,894

William's Age	Amount (PIA)
64	$2,446
65	$2,625
66 FRA	$2,764
67	$2,985
68	$3,206
69	$3,427
70	$3,648

Mary also had several options to choose from regarding income from her employer pension, which could begin when she turned sixty-five.

Mary also had a monthly income of approximately $1,305 from an inherited IRA.

Mary: Employer Pension Income Options	Amount
Single Life	$1,829
Joint Life with 50% Survivorship	$1,742
Joint Life with 100% Survivorship	$1,638

When choosing the right income plan, it is essential to consider longer life expectancy. This can require income to be stretched out for a longer period of time. Another area of concern is the loss of a spouse, and the income that is specific to him or her that could be lost. This income must be "replaced." Otherwise, the surviving spouse may have to drastically change his or her lifestyle.

Investment Management

The investment management portion of the plan consists of assessing risk tolerance, as well as adjusting—or converting—assets into income. In William and Mary's case, the couple had a variety of assets, including:

- William's employer-sponsored 401(k), as well as a 401(k) from a former employer
- Mary's 403(b) plan
- An IRA that Mary inherited from her mother
- Mary's Roth IRA
- A joint brokerage account
- A joint bank account
- The couple's home, which is currently valued at $415,000 and has a mortgage balance of less than $100,000

Tax Planning

Taxes are another primary component of an overall retirement plan. Even though future tax rates are unknown, it is essential to factor these in because they can significantly impact how much will be available to spend.

In many cases, including William and Mary, there will be a combination of both taxable and tax-free income in retirement. With that in mind, potential tax liability needs to be assessed, and an order of taking withdrawals must be established for tax efficiency.

Healthcare Planning and Wellness

One of a retiree's biggest expenses can be healthcare and long-term care. A recent Fidelity Investments study titled "How to Plan for Rising Healthcare Costs," concluded that a sixty-five-year-old couple who retired in 2021 can expect to pay approximately $300,000 in out-of-pocket healthcare costs during their remaining lifetimes—and that figure doesn't include long-term care.[34]

With that in mind, Medicare, Medicare Supplement, and long-term care coverage options need to be analyzed to reduce the strain on assets—particularly if assets and income generators are earmarked for other needs.

Legacy and Estate Management

When the time comes to transfer assets to the next generation, Uncle Sam could be the biggest beneficiary if a plan to minimize taxes is not in place. This includes strategies for reducing the

---

[34] Fidelity. Aug. 31, 2021. "How to plan for rising health care costs."
https://www.fidelity.com/viewpoints/personal-finance/plan-for-rising-health-care-costs.

future tax liability for children, grandchildren, and later generations.

Working with a retirement income professional, you will be able to see your whole financial picture as one, rather than individual components that have no correlation to one another. In fact, just like any well-run business, you should have a personal balance sheet that is regularly reviewed.

In the case of William and Mary, their balance sheet showed their assets, liabilities, and net worth in an easy-to-view format.

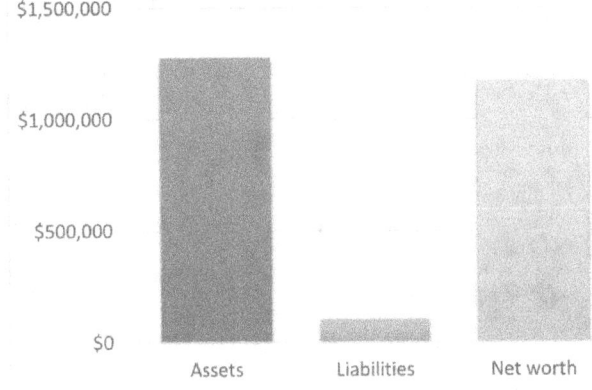

Your net worth is $1,173,387

Assets		Liabilities	
Bank	$34,448	Credit cards	$0
Invested assets	$827,643	Mortgages	$92,502
Real estate assets	$415,000	Home equities	$0
Life insurance cash value	$0	Student loans	$0
Other assets	$0	Other debts	$11,202
Total assets	**$1,277,091**	Total liabilities	**$103,704**
		Net worth	**$1,173,387**

Example shown for illustrative purposes only

It was further broken down into account types for assets, as well as the remaining balances that the couple had, which in this case, was the rest of their mortgage and one vehicle loan.

Balance Sheet Details

Description	William	Mary	Joint	Total
Assets				
Cash				
Joint bank account			$34,448	$34,448
Total cash	$0	$0	$34,448	$34,448
Invested assets				
Nonqualified				
Joint brokerage			$22,991	$22,991
Qualified				
William's current 401(k)	$375,715			$375,715
William's old 401(k)	$61,989			$61,989
Mary's 403(b)		$291,017		$291,017
William's current Roth 401(k)	$26,566			$26,566
Mary's Roth IRA		$16,452		$16,452
Mary's inherited IRA		$32,913		$32,913
Total investment assets	$464,270	$340,382	$22,991	$827,643
Real estate assets				
Primary home			$415,000	$415,000
Total real estate assets	$0	$0	$415,000	$415,000
Total assets	$464,270	$340,382	$472,439	$1,277,091
Liabilities				
Mortgage			$92,502	$92,502
Auto loan			$11,202	$11,202
Total liabilities	$0	$0	$103,704	$103,704

Example shown for illustrative purposes only

The advisor then reviewed the way William and Mary's assets were currently invested in order to determine if the way their assets were allocated was helping or hindering them from reaching their objectives.

The advisor determined that the couple was overweighted in equities, given their ages and their intended retirement date. Taking into consideration William and Mary's short- and long-term financial plan, the advisor proposed an allocation that was not as risky, while at the same time anticipated to give them a slightly higher return (without sleepless nights worrying about what will happen in the stock market).

Asset Allocation

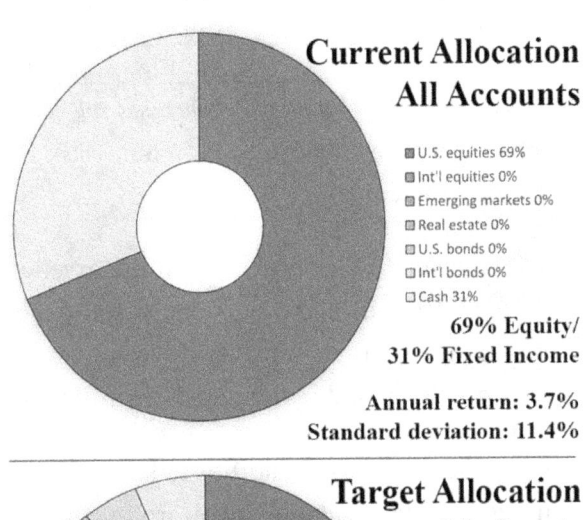

Current Allocation
All Accounts

- U.S. equities 69%
- Int'l equities 0%
- Emerging markets 0%
- Real estate 0%
- U.S. bonds 0%
- Int'l bonds 0%
- Cash 31%

**69% Equity/
31% Fixed Income**

Annual return: 3.7%
Standard deviation: 11.4%

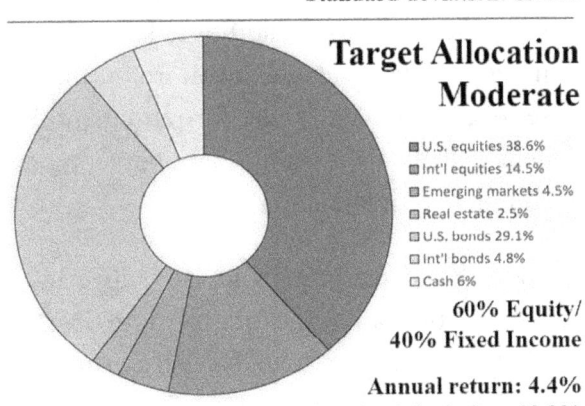

Target Allocation
Moderate

- U.S. equities 38.6%
- Int'l equities 14.5%
- Emerging markets 4.5%
- Real estate 2.5%
- U.S. bonds 29.1%
- Int'l bonds 4.8%
- Cash 6%

**60% Equity/
40% Fixed Income**

Annual return: 4.4%
Standard deviation: 10.2%

To balance back to your target portfolio:

U.S. Equities	Sell	$251,603
International Equities	Buy	$120,008
Emerging Markets	Buy	$37,244
Real Estate	Buy	$20,691
U.S. Bonds	Buy	$240,844
International Bonds	Buy	$39,727
Cash	Sell	$206,911

Example shown for illustrative purposes only and does not reflect any specific products or investments. Your actual situation will vary.

The advisor further broke down the asset allocation so that William and Mary could see exactly what percentage of their total assets were invested in—both currently and in the plan he was proposing.

Debt can hinder your ability to save for retirement. It can also take income away from other items and services you need to pay for retirement. Therefore, debt management should be a key component of a complete retirement plan.

So, William and Mary's advisor suggested that they use a debt management strategy to eliminate their mortgage and car loan balances. And, while this would require making a larger monthly payment now, it would free up funds that they could use for other needs (or wants) in retirement.

Debt Management Payments for William and Mary

(Example shown for illustrative purposes only)

(Proposed payments to begin next month)

Debt	Bal.	Int. Rate	Min. Pay	Curr. Pay	Prop. Pay
Mortg.	$92,502	3.725%	$1,616	$800	$1,616
Auto	$11,202	2.99%	$300	$300	$300

Debt management

Balance of Debt Selected

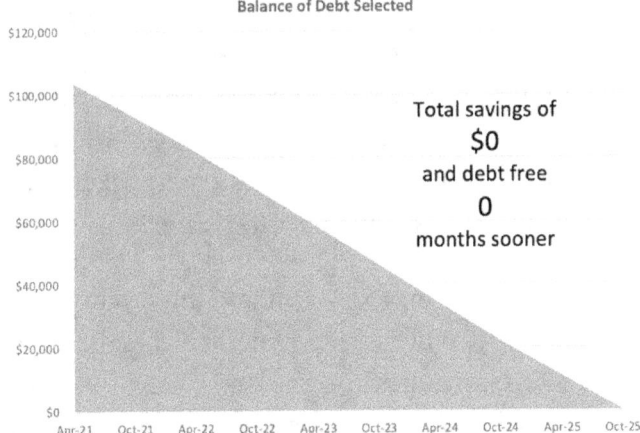

Total savings of $0 and debt free 0 months sooner

Proposed payment strategy

Payment priority	Same priority for all debt
Current total monthly payment	$1,916
Proposed additional monthly payment	$0
Proposed total monthly payment	$1,916

Individual loan strategy

Loan name	Interest rate	Balance	Strategy
Joint mortgage	3.725%	$92,502	Use proposed payment strategy
Joint car loan	2.99%	$11,202	Use proposed payment strategy

Another risk to your net spendable income in retirement is taxes. Sources from which you generate retirement income can play a key role in how much you keep in your own pocket and how much you must hand over to Uncle Sam.

Throughout the past hundred-plus years, the top federal income tax rate in the United States has fluctuated from a low of just 7 percent to a high of 94 percent. In forty-nine of the past 107 years, the top tax rate has been 70 percent or higher. So, you must have a plan for reducing or eliminating taxes in retirement.

Top Federal Income Tax Rates 1913 – 2020

YEAR	RATE	YEAR	RATE
2018-20	37	1950	84.36
2013-17	39.6	1948-49	82.13
2003-12	35	1946-47	86.45
2002	38.6	1944-45	94
2001	39.1	1942-43	88
1993-00	39.6	1941	81
1991-92	31	1940	81.1
1988-90	28	1936-37	79
1987	38.5	1932-35	63
1982-86	50	1930-31	25
1981	69.125	1929	24
1971-80	70	1925-28	25
1970	71.75	1924	46
1969	77	1923	43.5
1968	75.25	1922	58
1965-67	70	1919-21	73
1964	77	1918	77
1954-63	91	1917	67
1952-53	92	1916	15
1951	91	1913-15	7

Source: Inside Gov (http://federal-tax-rates.insidegov.com/)

There is a big difference between tax-deferred and tax-free. As its name suggests, tax-free means that you can access funds without having to pay tax—regardless of what your tax bracket at that time

On the other hand, tax-deferred simply means that taxes are postponed. In many cases, because the account balance is typically higher in the future, there is a higher taxable base. Take, for instance, money that is in a traditional IRA or 401(k) plan. Contributions are usually pre-tax, and the growth takes place tax-deferred. Therefore, 100 percent of your withdrawals will be taxable. In William and Mary's case, the bulk of their assets were situated in tax-deferred accounts.

William and Mary's Tax Allocation Summary

Taxable Asset
$22,991

Tax-deferred asset
$761,634

Tax-free asset
$43,018

Example shown for illustrative purposes only

Next, the advisor summarized the income that the couple could count on from their proposed sources. In this case, William and Mary would be receiving income from employer-sponsored pension plans, as well as Social Security.

While pension income remains the same throughout the years, Social Security could go up, based on the annual cost-of-living adjustment, or COLA. While this increase in Social Security income is not guaranteed, this program has raised the amount in all but just a few years throughout the program's history.

The income plan projected that both spouses would be receiving income for the first twenty-four years after retiring. He then proposed how the amount of income from Social Security would decrease following the death of one of the spouses. This, in turn, would reduce the total income inflows going forward.

Next, the advisor added in a plan for income distribution that the couple could take from employer-sponsored defined contribution plans (such as the traditional and Roth 401(k) plans, as well as the couple's IRA (Individual Retirement Accounts).

Factoring in expenses and tax payments, William and Mary would still have enough net spendable income to live a comfortable retirement lifestyle going forward. For an added measure of security, the advisor also proposed solutions for potential "high-ticket" expenses, such as the need for long-term care services and costly healthcare and medical needs.

In addition, even though the couple's estate was well below the estate tax exemption of $11.58 million (in 2020), the advisor still suggested that William and Mary consider putting various protections in force, such as an updated will, power of attorney, living wills, and healthcare proxy. That way, they could be assured that their wishes would be carried out.

Summary/Income Inflows

YEAR	AGE	SOCIAL SECURITY	PENSION	INCOME INFLOW
2021	65/63	0	0	0
2022	66/64	0	0	0
2023	67/65	0	19,656	19,656
2024	68/66	0	19,656	19,656
2025	69/67	0	19,656	19,656
2026	70/68	26,299	19,656	45,955
2027	71/69	45,536	19,656	65,192
2028	72/70	60,134	19,656	79,790
2029	73/71	80,735	19,656	100,391
2030	74/72	81,543	19,656	101,199
2031	75/73	82,358	19,656	102,014
2032	76/74	83,182	19,656	102,838
2033	77/75	84,013	19,656	103,669
2034	78/76	84,853	19,656	104,509
2035	79/77	85,702	19,656	105,358
2036	80/78	86,559	19,656	106,215
2037	81/79	87,425	19,656	107,081
2038	82/80	88,300	19,656	107,956
2039	83/81	89,181	19,656	108,837
2040	84/82	90,074	19,656	109,730
2041	85/83	90,975	19,656	110,631
2042	86/84	91,884	19,656	111,540
2043	87/85	92,802	19,656	112,458
2044	88/86	93,730	19,656	113,386
2045	89/87	94,668	19,656	114,324
2046	90/88	95,616	19,656	115,272
2047	91/89	55,562	19,656	75,218
2048	92/90	56,117	19,656	75,773

Example shown for illustrative purposes only

When you work with an experienced retirement income professional, you won't just be "sold" on "hot" investment tips or individual stocks that have no correlation to the rest of the portfolio. Rather, the advisor will review your whole picture in order to determine whether or not your current plan is likely to be successful, or if there is another route that could do better.

Upon reviewing William and Mary's current portfolio and then comparing it with a new proposed plan that took into consideration the couple's current and anticipated future situation, there was a significant difference in the probability of success.

If you were William and Mary, which plan would you choose?

Proposed plan

Current plan

Hypothetical example shown for illustrative purposes only and does not represent any specific products or investments, nor does it ensure financial success. Your actual portfolio will vary.

SEVEN

Taking the Next Step

As you approach retirement, there are a number of concerns you may have regarding your money. These can include the following:

- **Market Volatility:** Keeping your principal protected in an uncertain stock market.

- **Inflation:** Not being able to keep your retirement income on pace with the future rising costs of goods and services you need over time.

- **Order of Returns:** Obtaining negative returns either at or just before you begin to take retirement income withdrawals. This can have a substantial effect on how long your income—and even the total amount of money in your overall portfolio—lasts.

- **Low Returns:** In an effort to keep principal protected, some investors take a "flight to safety" approach and move funds into vehicles such as CDs, bonds, or even bank savings accounts. Unfortunately, while you won't actually "lose" money in these vehicles, what can happen is you lose future purchasing power—over time, that can have a significantly negative impact on your lifestyle and even on your life overall.

- **Taxes**: The taxes you pay on your investment gains and on your income can also be a concern. This is because taxes can essentially erode your total return over time.

- **Health and Long-Term Care Expenses**: Although most people don't want to discuss it, there is a high probability of needing at least some type of long-term care services at some time in your life after reaching age sixty-five—these services can be expensive. So, the best thing to do is to plan ahead, so the funds you may require don't disrupt your retirement savings or your retirement income.

- **Longevity:** Our longer lives today, while a blessing for many people, can also mean we must take a different approach to our long-term financial and retirement income planning if we want our funds to last for the twenty, thirty, or more years we may spend in retirement. This is because living longer exposes us to all of the above risks for a longer period of time.

With so many things to be aware of, it can make income planning confusing. On the one hand, you want to keep your hard-earned principal protected. Yet, at the same time, you don't want to risk gaining too low of returns on your money and end up losing future purchasing power.

Trying to plan around all of these potential obstacles can often make investors act illogically—and it's easy to see why. For example, when the stock market is going up, you want to take advantage of "bargain" prices. Yet, just as quickly as it goes up, the market can also go down and wipe out all of your profits—and then some.

Having a system in place that can step you through the "whats," the "hows," and the "whens" would make things much easier—and that's just how the time-based segmentation system can help. This is because the time-based segmentation system provides an actual plan for you to follow.

This step-by-step plan sets out what you need to help address:

- Reducing uncertainty
- Bridging income gaps
- Keeping income on pace with inflation
- Preparing for health/long-term care expenses
- Paying estate taxes

The best way to ensure you will have the retirement lifestyle you hoped for is to plan ahead for it. With the time-based segmentation system, you will be able to do just that.

If what you've read here makes you want to learn more about your own retirement options, we'd be delighted to talk to you and discuss how we can help.

Artie Bernaducci & Denny Frasiolas
Retirement Income Advisory Group, LLC
Phone: (732) 455-9990
Email: info@retire-usa.com
www.retire-usa.com

About Retirement Income Advisory Group

Financial planning is all about helping you address the "what-ifs" in life. Your retirement income is where we start the planning process.

Whether you are ten years away from retirement or ten years into retirement, we begin the planning process with a retirement income assessment.

We've found our clients enjoy the confidence of knowing where their next retirement paycheck will come from.

There's no such thing as a perfect investment, but we strive to create the right mix of strategies for your particular situation. These strategies help to streamline the process, remove the complication, and keep your goals and plans on track.

We consider it a privilege to provide a broad range of services to meet the varying needs of our clients.

We understand your goals and dreams can't be reached with a cookie-cutter approach. Thus, our services are uniquely tailored to address your specific concerns.

Our Mission

Our mission is to help keep clients from unknowingly and unnecessarily depleting their retirement savings and to create strategies designed to minimize the chances clients outlive their money.

About Artie Bernaducci

Artie Bernaducci is the founder of Retirement Income Advisory Group, LLC, and he has been working in his favorite profession since 1991.

Throughout his career, his priority has been to help clients understand financial gobbledygook and help make it simpler for them to plan their retirement.

He quickly found effective ways to communicate so people could respond to sound advice and help improve their situation, instead of doing nothing about their future.

He has often stated, "It was no fun to try and help someone while I used language that caused their eyes to glaze over!"

After graduating from Ball State University in Indiana with a Bachelor of Science degree in soil science, he was unable to find work in his major area of study, so he went into the masonry business with his family and ran his own successful company for more than a decade.

The masonry business had its own gobbledygook. Despite a steep learning curve, Artie worked hard to simplify the language for day-to-day business.

With his transition to the financial world, it was a given he would apply this same approach and ensure clients could understand the industry "mumbo jumbo" to move forward with planning their retirement.

Artie is passionate about helping people and enjoys connecting with his clients. His focus includes retirement and financial income planning, and he especially enjoys assisting baby boomers approaching, or are already in, retirement. He is also a licensed insurance professional.

His aim is to educate clients and support them with the retirement knowledge they need to journey through their life stages.

He has co-authored the book ***The Baby Boomer Retirement Roadmap*** with his colleague Denny Frasiolas. He also speaks on retirement and financial income planning at many seminars.

Artie is married to his best friend and wife, Monica. He has four adult children: Rosaleen, Nicole, Jessica, and Louis; as well as four grandsons. Artie's main interests are family, bodybuilding, yoga, meditation, marketing, veganism, and "paying it forward."

About Denny Frasiolas

Denny Frasiolas is the managing partner and chief investment officer at Retirement Income Advisory Group, LLC, and he has been a financial professional since 2001.

He focuses on addressing clients' (with an emphasis on baby boomers) biggest concerns about wealth distribution planning and IRA/401(k) investment services. He's also an author, speaker, business consultant, and entrepreneur.

Denny knew he wanted a career in financial planning after he helped a family member who unexpectedly lost a loved one. He took responsibility to restore order and created a financial plan working to their benefit and helping them save more toward their retirement nest egg.

When things suddenly change in life and there's no plan in place, you often have to scramble to figure things out, and Denny doesn't want others to experience that.

He holds a B.S. degree in finance and a B.S. degree in operations management from Indiana University's Kelley School of Business, and he is also a licensed insurance professional. He received his master's degree in mathematics education from The College of New Jersey.

In addition, he has held several highly regarded positions in his professional career, including positions at Bank of America (formerly Fleet Bank), as a financial analyst, and at MetLife, as an investment advisor representative.

Denny has co-authored or contributed to three books with his colleague Artie Bernaducci: ***Strategies to Create Lifetime Income for Baby Boomers*** (2016), ***Financially Empowered, Taking***

Charge of Your Financial Life (2018), and ***The Baby Boomer Retirement Roadmap*** (2020).

He is devoted to improving people's financial literacy and has spoken to the general public about retirement and financial income planning, Social Security, Medicare, and identity theft.

He's also been a guest at several corporations, speaking to insurance agency sales force personnel, attorneys, certified public accountants, financial advisors, and insurance agents.

Denny is also the co-founder of All Access Brokerage, LLC, which manages employee benefits and offers Medicare education and enrollment services for families in New York, New Jersey, and Pennsylvania.

He was a past chapter president of the 501(c)(3) nonprofit public benefit corporation, The Society for Financial Awareness (SOFA).

At the center of Denny's life is his beautiful wife, Erin, as well as their three wonderful children: Parker, Mason, and Charlotte.

www.ingramcontent.com/pod-product-compliance
Lightning Source LLC
Chambersburg PA
CBHW060850220526
45466CB00003B/1319